How-To-Draw
Exotic Cars

Steve Schmor

Order this book online at www.trafford.com
or email orders@trafford.com

Most Trafford titles are also available at major online book retailers.

Print information available on the last page.

ISBN: 978-1-4120-3766-2 (sc)

Trafford rev. 10/11/2022

Trafford PUBLISHING®   www.trafford.com
North America & international
toll-free: 844-688-6899 (USA & Canada)
fax: 812 355 4082

Acknowledgements

I thank GOD for giving me the vision and talent to write this book and to bless others with this artistic knowledge.

I also want to thank my wife, Aurelia and family for standing by me with this vision and supporting me through this project. I sincerely hope it helps you in achieving your artistic goals, whether small or great. And that you use this book as a tool to run with **your** vision and artistic talents.

Preface

This book was created for people who love to draw cars. By using the method explained in this book you will be able to draw more than just these exotic cars. I chose these cars because, let's face it, almost every kid I've known including myself have either had a poster or a model of these cars. If you are like me you would have had both.

Completely read the Introduction to this book and refer to it often. The process explained in the Introduction will guide you through what to look for, how to measure lines and angles and terms you need to know when drawing. It will also help you to train your brain and see detail instead of complete objects.

Most people loose their drawing ability at around the age of nine or ten. This is because they are learning more essential information for everyday use like language and math skills. The ability for people to draw is still there it just needs to be tapped into and developed. I believe anyone can pick up a pencil and regain their drawing skills using this technique, these examples and of course "practice". Anyone can draw a straight line, square, triangle or a circle. If you can draw these simple shapes then YOU CAN DRAW!

Introduction

Read all of the information in the introduction and practice the examples first before attempting the car exercises in this book. The techniques described in this book are centuries old yet simple and practical for drawing anything. At first you may think that these exercises are too difficult. With practice you will be able to draw professionally using the technique described in the next few pages. When you start any drawing make **<u>light</u>** lines first because you may need to erase and adjust the angles of your lines. Don't think erasing is bad. Even "professionals" need to erase from time to time. When you have the angles and proportions correct for your drawing go back over your drawing with your pencil and make darker lines to sharpen the detail and identify the darker areas. I hope you enjoy learning from the exercises in this book as much as I enjoyed making it. Remember the more you practice the better you will be able to draw. And of course you should always have fun!

Using this book

When doing the car exercises, refer to the picture at the beginning of each exercise as the example you are to draw. The steps described for each car exercise are in the same measurements and proportion as the picture at the beginning of each exercise.

Materials:

- **Blank paper** (Most any paper will do)

- **Pencils** (A regular HB pencil will do for the most part and a mechanical pencil for fine detail)

- **Eraser** (a white plastic eraser is the best and can be cut to a sharp edge to erase fine detail)

- **Pencil sharpener** (Any pencil sharpener will do but the metal ones do a better job at creating that perfect point)

Things to know

Proportion: The size of one part of the picture in relation to the size of another part. In other words proportion is what dictates that, in drawing cars, side windows are not as high as the height of the car. If proportion is not correct in a drawing it "doesn't look right."

Perspective: This is the illusion that the further away things are the smaller they seem to be and the closer things are the bigger they seem to be.

Measuring: This is a method used by many artists. Artists use an object like a paint brush, their thumb or pencil to determine the relationship between the distance between lines and areas of what they are drawing (proportion).

Base Measure: Find a good straight line from the picture you are drawing and measure it with your pencil (see Using a pencil to measure below). This will help you with finding lengths of lines and distances between lines within your drawing. You can use this common line as a base measurement or what is known as a base measure. Using this base measure to compare to other lines will help you find the proportion of your drawing.

*Two things to look for are the **length of lines** and the **angles of these lines** in relation to the horizontal and vertical viewpoints of what you are drawing.*

Using a pencil to measure:

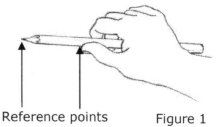

- Hold the pencil in your hand with your thumb free to slide along the pencil for your second point of reference (see Figure 1 at right).

Reference points   Figure 1

- Close one eye if needed (to get an accurate measurement). Hold the pencil along the line that you have chosen to measure with the tip of your pencil as the first reference point for that line.

- By holding your pencil still on this line, slide your thumb along your pencil to the other end of this same line. **You now have a measurement for this line**.

- Hold your thumb at this place on your pencil and place your pencil flat on your paper at the same angle of the line you just measured (see figure 2).

- Make a mark on your blank paper at the tip of your pencil. Keeping the pencil flat on the paper with the tip on your mark note where your thumb is and then put another mark at this point. Now draw a line between these two points.

Blank paper

Make your reference
points and then draw a
line between them.

Figure 2

Tip: Keep your arm at the same distance when measuring to ensure your proportions are correct.

Let's do the example of the line below. Place your pencil flat on the line drawn below with the tip at one end of the line. Now slide your thumb across the pencil until it is at the other end of this line. These will be your two reference points. Hold your thumb in this position on your pencil and place your pencil at the same angle on your blank paper. Make a mark with the tip of your pencil. Keeping your pencil flat on the paper on this first mark put your finger from your opposite hand at the point where your thumb is on your pencil. Make a mark where you placed your finger and then draw a line between these two marks. You should have drawn a line that looks similar to the one below.

Example

In any drawing, you want to find a **base measure** and use it as your main measurement. This will help you identify the proportion for the other lines you are drawing for your picture. You also want to find the whole area that your picture will use. Do this by measuring the length, height and width of your picture and lightly draw a box or small boundary points on your blank paper for this area (see figure 3 below). This will also help to keep your picture in proportion.

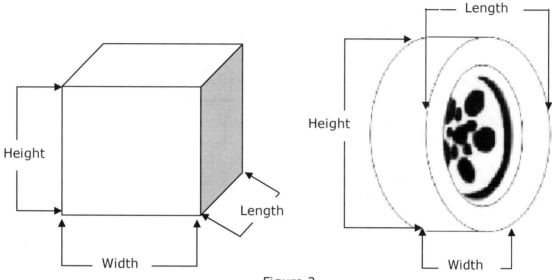

Figure 3

Practice by drawing the wheel below. Measure the length, height and width of the picture below left. First lightly draw a box or small boundary points to identify the area the wheel will occupy. Next measure the dotted arrows for the front part of the tire "A" and make reference marks with your pencil on your blank paper at these points. Now connect the marks you just made by drawing an oval. You should have something that looks like "B."

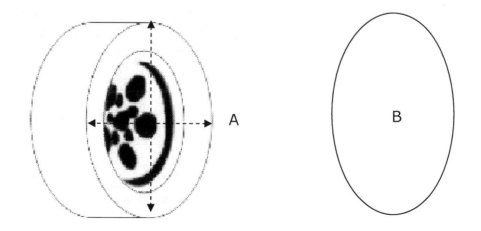

Measure the distance between the two ovals for the thickness of the tire, see "C" below. From these new points of reference, draw a second oval just to the left of the one you just finished drawing, see "D" below. Draw a **light** solid line (not dotted).

Tip: The farther apart your ovals are the wider your tire will look.

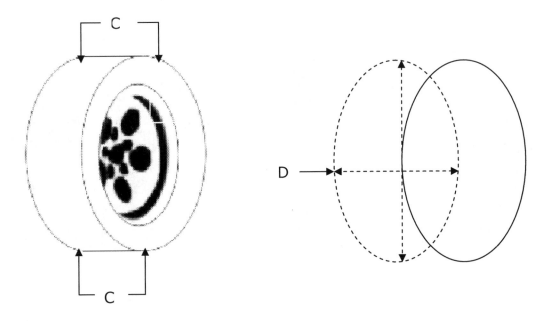

Next draw the top and bottom of your tire with straight lines (not dotted), see "E" below.

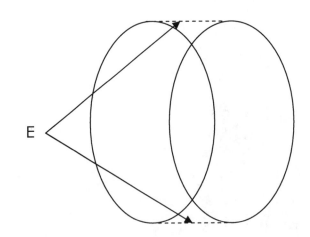

Sometimes it is necessary to erase lines that don't belong. Carefully erase the unwanted lines inside the tire (see the dotted lines for "F").

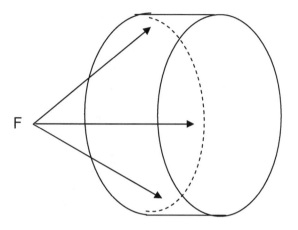

F

Now add a smaller oval inside the first oval you drew, see "G."

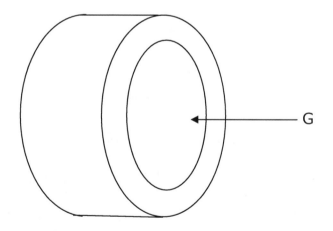

G

Add the details of the inner oval by drawing and shading different sized circles and ovals to add depth, (see the black areas of the wheel for "H"). Add the shaded curve "I" by following the outline of the inner oval you drew previously for step "G." Be careful not to make this detail too large. You now have a basic tire and rim. Practice this technique by drawing different tires from other pictures you find.

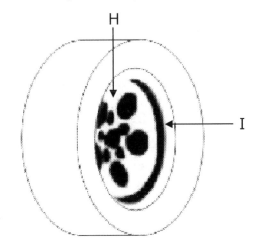

Once you can draw these simple shapes you are well on your way to piece together all kinds of pictures.

Checking for proportion

Do the following to ensure your drawing is in proportion:

1) **Measure the length, width and height of the sample picture and** compare it to yours.
2) **Measure the width of a wheel through the center and see how many** wheel widths a car is and then compare this to your drawing (this is good for side views).
3) **Use other reference points from the picture you are drawing to double** check that your lines are in the correct place. Using different reference points between lines will help keep your drawing in proportion. This will also help insure the angles are correct.

Tip: When you start a new picture make sure your first line is in a good *spot on your blank paper. Otherwise your drawing will get too close to the edge of your page or it will end up going completely off your paper.*

The Brain

Understanding how your brain works may help you to identify detail. Your brain works in two basic ways, **Verbal** and **Visual**. When you look at a tire, the **Verbal** side of your brain tells you quickly that this is a tire. Your **Visual** side tells you that this curved line joins this straight line and in the middle there are some circles and oval shapes. Most of us have been trained to interpret things verbally as to what they are as complete objects; we translate these objects with our **Verbal** brain faster thus, canceling out the individual shapes. When drawing you want to look for these shapes, not the name of the picture you are drawing. If you find you are having difficulty processing what you see flip the picture you are drawing upside down. This tricks your brain into canceling out your **Verbal** side and seeing lines and shapes rather than the name of the object. This will also help you to see more detail and be a better artist.

Time to get started

The first car exercise in this book has lots of instruction, similar to the previous tire exercise. The remaining exercises will have new lines to draw with instructions where needed. The trickier lines, such as small curves, are in magnified areas for a closer view. Some steps are numbered to do in a particular order.

With some practice you will be able to draw these cars easily. With even more practice you will be able to draw different cars from pictures, look at a real car and draw them or design your own dream car.

Like I mentioned...

ANYONE CAN DRAW!

Table of Contents

Lamborghini Countach

General Information

Price:	$85,000 + U.S.
Miles per Gallon:	11 mpg
Curb Weight:	2645 lbs
Layout:	Mid-Engine/RWD
Transmission:	5-Speed Manual

Engine

Type:	V12
Displacement:	3929 cc
Horsepower:	353 @ 7500 rpm
Torque:	267 lb-ft @ 5500 rpm

Performance

0-60 mph:	5.9 sec
0-100 mph:	14.4 sec
Quarter Mile:	14.6 sec @ 101 mph
Top Speed:	180 mph

Let's start with an easy car to draw. The Lamborghini Countach is an easy car to draw because it is made up of a lot of straight lines.

When you start drawing a picture make light lines because you may need to erase and correct a line from time to time. You can make your lines darker after you have completed your picture to show more detail but for now don't make them too dark.

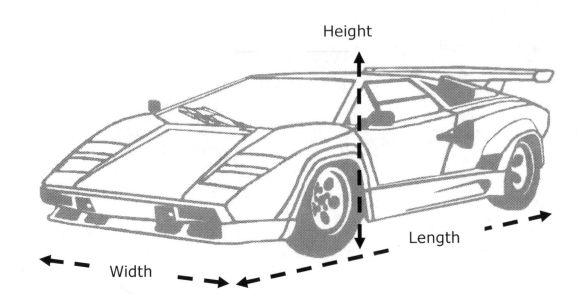

Height

Length

Width

Measure the dotted lines to find the general area (length, width and height) for your picture. You can make small marks for these boundaries that you can erase later. This will help you stay in the boundaries and keep your picture in proportion. This also means that your first line was in the right place on your page.

Start with the top of the windshield as a **base measure**. The top of a windshield is usually a good place to start as it is usually fairly straight. Use the length of this measurement to compare it to the rest of the car, being aware of the angles. Measure the top of the windshield and draw it at the same angle on your blank paper. Make sure you draw this line in an area on your paper that will leave room to fit the rest of your drawing.

A ———————————— B

Next measure between the bottom left corner of the windshield point "C" and the top left point "A" from the picture you are using to draw from. Make a small mark on your paper at this point. Join these points together to make the line for the left of the windshield. You can double check that the angle is correct by measuring between point "C" and point "B".

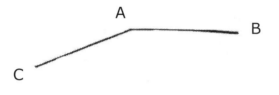

Draw the other side of the windshield by measuring from point "B" to point "D". Make a small mark at point "D" and draw a line between these points. Remember you can double check the angle by measuring from point "C" to point "D" and from point "A" to point "D".

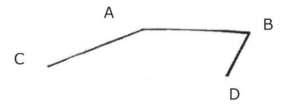

Measure between point "C" and point "E" and make a small mark.
Draw a line between these points to connect the dots. Make sure you
double check to see if this angle is correct by measuring from point "B"
to point "E".

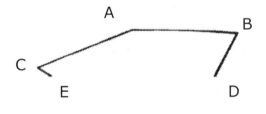

Now draw the bottom of the windshield by making a measurement
from point "E" to point "F", making a mark and then draw a line.
Double check this point by measuring from pint "B" to point "F" or
point "A" to point "F".

**Find reference point as you continue with your drawing to
assure that your angles are correct.**

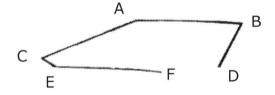

The last line of the windshield is a little different because it has a little curve to it. You already have the reference points so you don't need to measure you just need to get the curve correct. Draw the curved line to join the last two points together and you will have completed the windshield.

Next measure and draw the front of your car. Measure the distance from point "A" to point "B" and make a mark at point "B". DO NOT draw a line between these two marks. Then measure the distance from point "C" to point "D" and make another mark at point "D". DO NOT draw a line between these two marks. Now draw a line between "B" and "D". You have now started the front of your car. You can check the angles of these lines by measuring between points "A" and "D" and points "C" and "B".

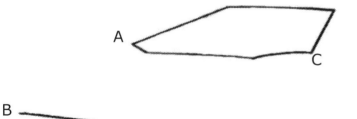

This next step has a few more lines involved. Make a measurement from point "A" to point "B" for the left fender and draw a curved line between these points. ***Note that the line at point "A" sticks out a little bit*** (see the expanded view in the circle below). Now measure from point "B" to point "C" make a mark and draw a line between the mark for "C" and point "D". Do the same for the other side by measuring from point "E" to point "F." Make another mark at point "F" and draw a line between points "F" and "G". Draw a curved line between point "F" and point "G". Draw a curved line between "E" and "H" (note that you will have to measure or estimate the little line between "H" - see the arrow for "H" below). Now draw in the lines for "I" (measure these lines if you need to but you should be able to see where they should go easily enough).

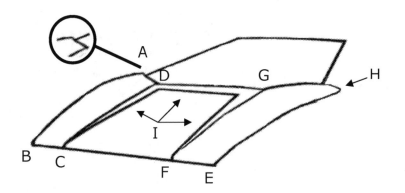

Draw a line from the top left side of the windshield **here** to that little spot that sticks out **here**.
This will be the door frame for the left side of your car

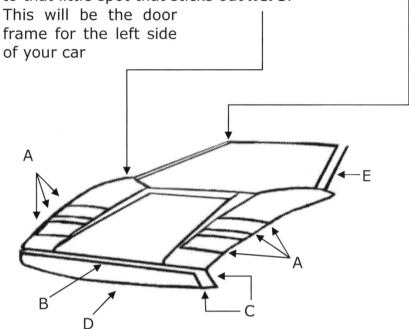

Draw the four lines for the two headlights "A" on each side of the front. Draw a parallel line below the one at the front of the car "B" and add the two little angled lines to the right side of each of these lines "C". Now join these angled lines for "C" together. Draw a bowed line "D" to complete the nose of your car. Measure the same distance from top and bottom of the right side of the windshield and draw a parallel line for the beginning of the door "E".

Now continue with the door. We will come back and finish the front later. Measure between points "A" and "B" and make a mark for each of these points and then draw your line for the top of the door. Make sure to get the angle correct. Now measure between points "C" and "D" and draw a curved line. You can double check this angle by measuring between points "A" and "D". Next make another measurement and add the line between points "D" and "E". You can double check this angle by measuring between points "B" and "E". This line should be parallel to the top of the door. Finally make your last measurement between "E" and "F" and draw a line. Draw a line between the last points "B" and "F" noting the small curve close to point "F".

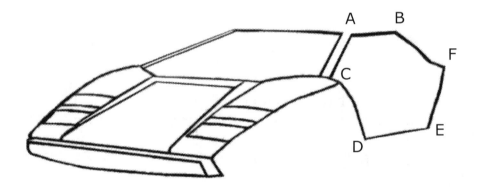

To draw the curve in the roof, measure from the top right corner of the windshield to the top of the roof "C" and make a light mark. Draw a curved line between points "A" and "B" through the mark for "C". Measure between points "B" and "D" and draw a **light** curved line. Next add the bent part to the line between "B" and "D" (see the expanded view in the circle below). Measure and add the small curved line below "D" for the back of the car. Now draw a line from the middle of the door to the back of the car "E" (just above "D"). Measure between the double arrows "F" and make two marks and then draw the line for the bottom of the car. Double check the line for the bottom of the car to see if it is correct by measuring between the dotted arrows.

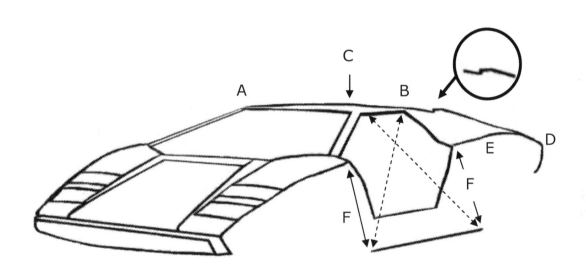

Draw a curved line from the bottom left corner of the windshield to the back of the car "A" through the middle of the door. Now draw a second line just below the line you just drew and continue it all the way to the back of the car "A". Draw the lines for the window "B". Following the diagram add the door handle "C" and an extra line from the door handle to the back of the car (see the arrow for "C" below).

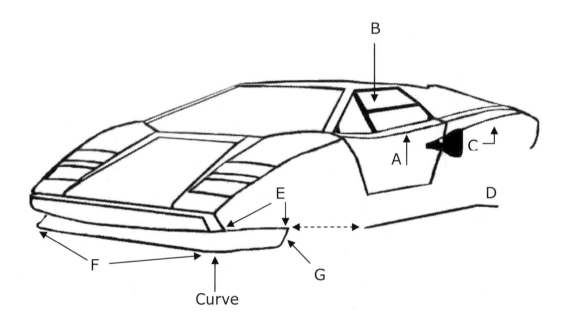

Measure and draw the small line for "D" assuring that the angle is correct. This will be the beginning of the back wheel well. Measure between the arrows for "E" and draw the small line for the front the car. You can double check the length of line "E" by measuring from the right end of "E" to the bottom of the car (see the dotted arrow). Next measure and draw the small line at the left of "F" and continue this line for "F" to the bottom of "E" noting the curve (see arrow). Join the line between "E" and "F" together with "G".

Now it's time to complete the wheel wells. For the back wheel well draw a half oval but draw the back of the oval a little below the back end of the car (see the arrow for "A" below). You can assure the measurement is correct by measuring from the back of the car down to the arrow for "A". Draw another half oval for the front wheel well "B". Now draw another line similar just above the last one you drew for "B". Add a third wheel well line for "C" but only draw it above the bottom front to the top right of the wheel well. Connect the two wheel wells together with line "D" by measuring up from each end of the bottom car line (the line connecting the two wheel wells together) and draw the line just below the door "D". Draw another line just above "A" for line "E".

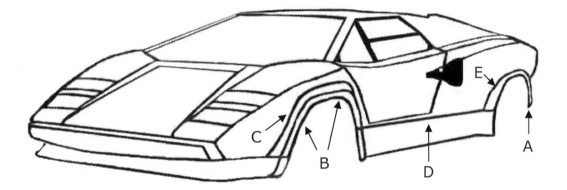

Now you are ready to add the wing. Measure up from the top left of
the door window "A" to the roof line and make a small mark. Next
measure from the back of the car to the arrow for "B" and make
another mark. Now draw a line between points "A" and "B". Make a
mark at "C" and another mark at "D" and then draw a line between "C"
and "D" for the bottom of the wing. Next draw an oval for the end of
the wing "E" (draw the back side of the oval with a straight line with a
rounded point – see the arrow for "E" below). Now add the top line for
the wing "F" noting that it doesn't go straight across (the left side
curves in towards the roof at "A" – see the arrow for "F" below).

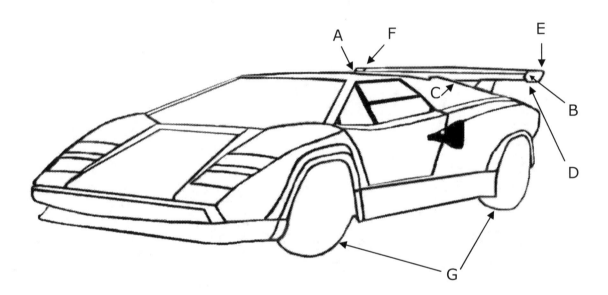

Add the bottom of the wheels by drawing half circles for "G" noting
where they connect to the car.

Now for the final touches. You can do this last step in any order you like. Here is a suggested order. Following the diagram add the mirrors and windshield wiper "A" and shade them in. Shade in the area for the rear vent "B" (see details below before the vent was shading – think of the vent as a triangle and rectangle). Draw a curved line over the rear wheel well and a short line from the back of the door then add a little square for "C". Shade in the square for "C". At the bottom of the door draw two lines for "D" with the shorter line on top and a longer line slightly below. Now add a small quarter circle and shade it in. For the rims lightly draw an oval slightly inside from the outer edge of each tire (you can measure from each side, top and bottom of the tire to get the proportions correct). Fill in the center of the rims with small circles and ovals as shown below and shade them in. Next draw a thick curved half circle inside each rim on the right side for a shadow. Finally add shaded areas to the front of the car "E" as shown below for the lights and air flow holes.

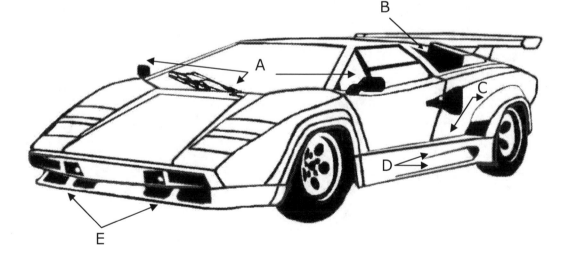

Congratulations! You have just finished drawing a Lamborghini Countach. With a little practice you will be drawing this car and others in this book with ease impressing your friends with your awesome super machines.

Ferrari F40

General Information

Price:	$400,000 U.S.
Miles per Gallon:	24 mpg
Curb Weight:	2976 lbs
Layout:	Mid-Engine/RWD
Transmission:	5-Speed Manual

Engine

Type:	Twin-Turbo V8
Displacement:	2936 cc
Horsepower:	478 @ 7000 rpm
Torque:	424 lb-ft @ 4500 rpm

Performance

0-60 mph:	3.8 sec
0-100 mph:	8.0 sec
Quarter Mile:	11.8 sec @ 124 mph
Top Speed:	201 mph

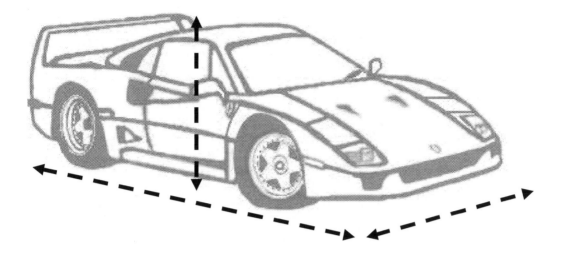

Again use these guide lines to find the general area of your picture.

Tip: *Reference the drawings often to make sure you are on the right track with your measurements and placing of lines and detail.*

Start with the top of the windshield in a comfortable spot on your page.

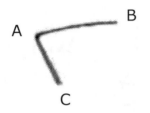

Measure and draw the left line for the windshield "C".

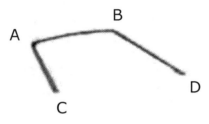

Measure and draw the right line for the windshield "D".

Draw the bottom line for the windshield by connecting the two sides together.

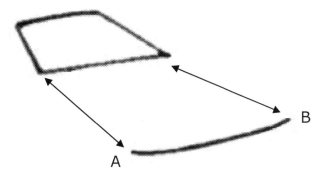

Measure between the arrows and make marks for the curved line for the front of the car. Draw the line between points "A" and "B" with a slight curve to it.

Measure in from the front right side of the car and make a mark. Now draw the right line for the hood of the car from this point to the right corner of the windshield.

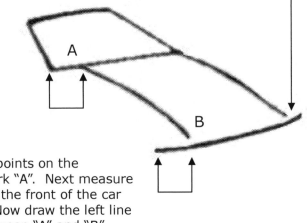

Measure between the two points on the windshield and make a mark "A". Next measure between the two points on the front of the car and make a mark at "B". Now draw the left line for the hood of the car between "A" and "B".

Measure the distance between the curved and straight line at this point and draw this curved line from the front of the car to the bottom right of the windshield.

B

Draw a curved line between "A" and "B" and then erase the small space at the arrow for "A".

You can double check the top end of this line at point "B" by measuring between the bottom left of the windshield to point "B".

A

Draw the two small front lines for the bottom of the headlights.

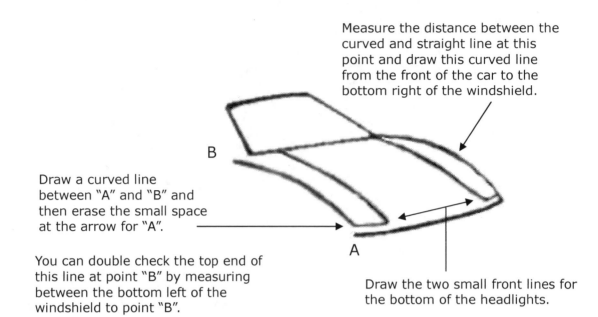

1)   Measure from the bottom left corner of the windshield to this point and draw this line first.

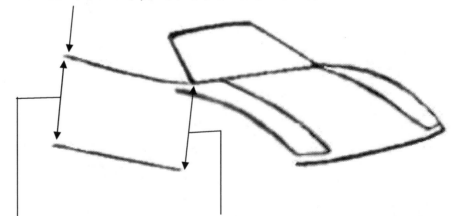

2)   Measure between the double arrows and draw the line for the bottom of the car. This line should be parallel to the bottom of the door window. The front arrow is measured from the corner of the windshield.

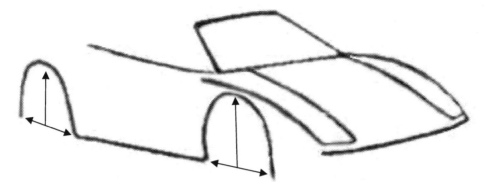

Measure the width and height for the wheel wells and make marks at the ends of the arrows. Now draw a half circle for each wheel well.

Measure and finish drawing the side window "A".

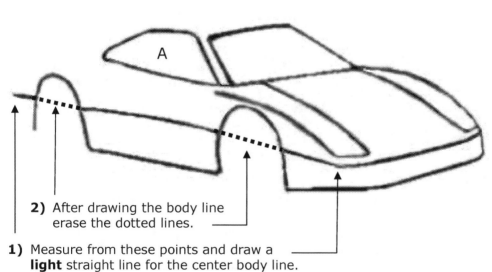

2) After drawing the body line erase the dotted lines.

1) Measure from these points and draw a **light** straight line for the center body line.

3) Draw a line between these points **last** for the bottom of the wing.

1) Measure from the top left corner of the windshield to this point and make a mark to get the curve for the roof correct then draw the roof line around to the back of the side window.

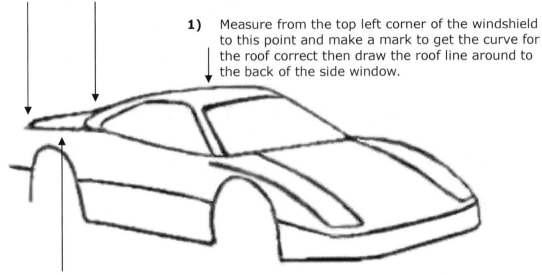

2) Measure and extend this line for the back.

3) Connect the line for the top of the wing and curve it down on the right side to join the point for step two.

2) Measure from the top right of the windshield to this point and make a mark for the right side of the wing.

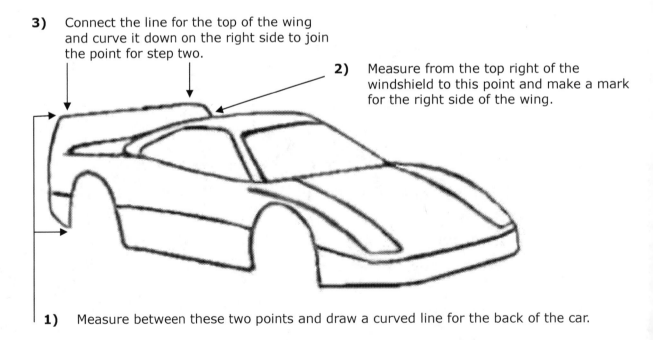

1) Measure between these two points and draw a curved line for the back of the car.

3) Connect the tops of the two small lines you just drew to complete the wing.

2) Measure the small inner line for this side of the wing and draw it (noting the angle).

1) Measure from this corner up to the inside corner of this side of the wing and draw this line.

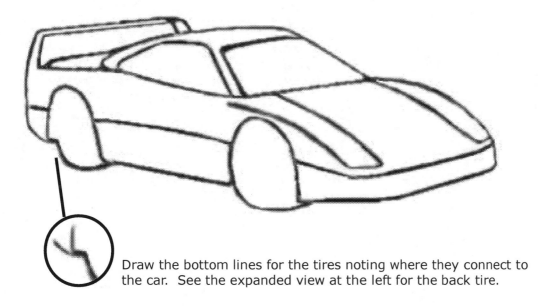

Draw the bottom lines for the tires noting where they connect to the car. See the expanded view at the left for the back tire.

Draw an oval for the back rim and a circle for the front rim and then fill them in as shown. Note that the front wheel is supposed to look turned in. See the steps below for building the front rim.

Draw a circle with two circles in the middle.

Draw a partial circle just inside the left side.

Draw five triangles to form a star and add dots around the inner circle just outside of the triangles.

Shade in a small triangle for the rear air
intake and the back part of the side window

Draw the mirrors and
windshield wiper.

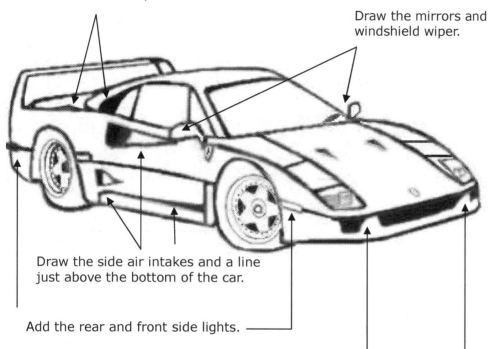

Draw the side air intakes and a line
just above the bottom of the car.

Add the rear and front side lights. ———

Draw the four lines on the hood for the front lights and the detail
for the bottom lights. Add two shaded triangles for the hood
intakes and shade in the front air intakes at the bottom of the car.

Shade in the tires and add the lines for the door. Enjoy your picture.

Jaguar XJ220

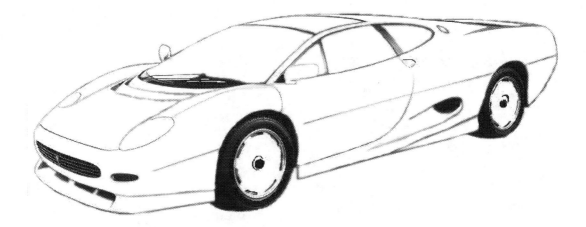

General Information
Price:	$700,000 + U.S.
Miles per Gallon:	13.1 mpg
Curb Weight:	3241 lbs
Layout:	Mid-Engine/RWD
Transmission:	5-Speed Manual

Engine
Type:	Twin-Turbo V6
Displacement:	3494 cc
Horsepower:	542 bhp @ 7200 rpm
Torque:	475 lb-ft @ 4500 rpm

Performance
0-60 mph:	3.8 sec
0-100 mph:	7.3 sec
Quarter Mile:	11.9 sec @ 122 mph
Top Speed:	217 mph

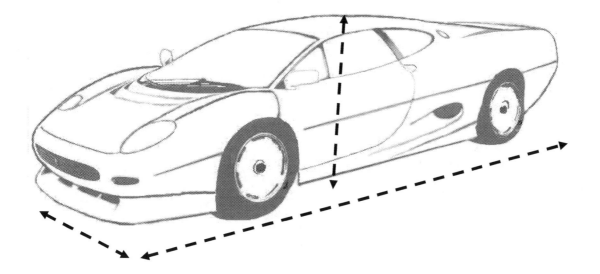

This car is more challenging because there are less straight lines and a lot of curved lines. Measure the area your car will use and mark off your boundaries.

A  B

Start your first line by drawing the top of the windshield.

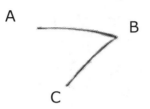

Measure between "B" and "C" and draw the right side of the windshield.

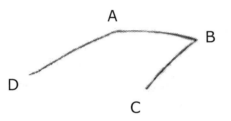

Now measure between "A" and "D" and draw the left side of the windshield.

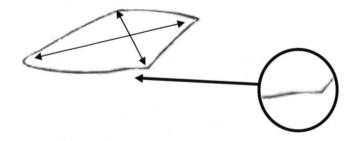

Complete the windshield by closing the bottom with a curved line. Note the small curve on the right (see the expanded view). You can double check your angles by measuring between opposite corners of the windshield (see the arrows inside the windshield).

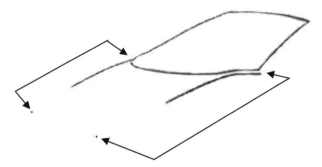

Measure from the bottom corners on each side of the windshield to the black dots and draw these two black dots. Do not erase these marks as you will need them later. Then draw the two short lines as shown inline with these dots. Note that that the right line has a curve at the right side of it.

Draw the curved line for the left fender from the left side of the windshield to the front left dot you drew in the previous step. Measure the distance between the double arrows to get the curve correct for the left fender.

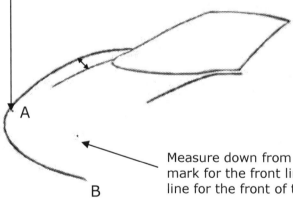

Measure down from the right dot to point "B" and make a mark for the front line to join. Then continue the curved line for the front of the car from point "A" to point "B".

Measure from the top left corner of the windshield to this point and draw the curved line for the roof.

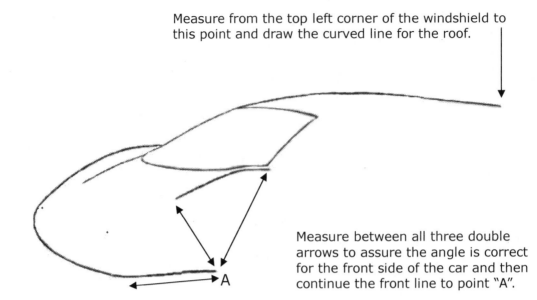

Measure between all three double arrows to assure the angle is correct for the front side of the car and then continue the front line to point "A".

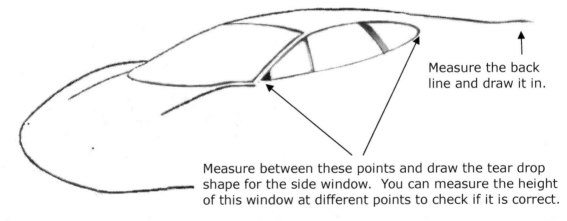

Measure the back line and draw it in.

Measure between these points and draw the tear drop shape for the side window. You can measure the height of this window at different points to check if it is correct.

Then add the two lines to separate it into three windows with a small shaded triangle at the front of this window.

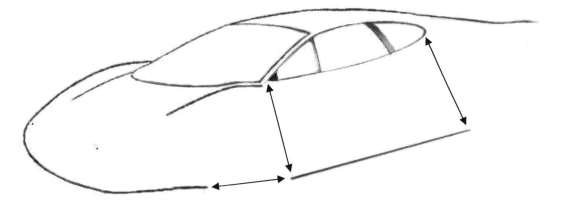

Measure between the double arrows and draw the bottom of the car.

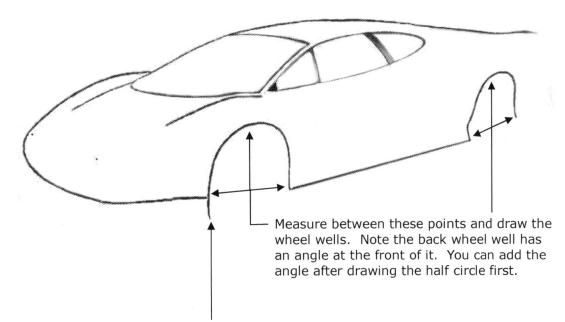

Measure between these points and draw the wheel wells. Note the back wheel well has an angle at the front of it. You can add the angle after drawing the half circle first.

Measure and draw an extend line downwards.

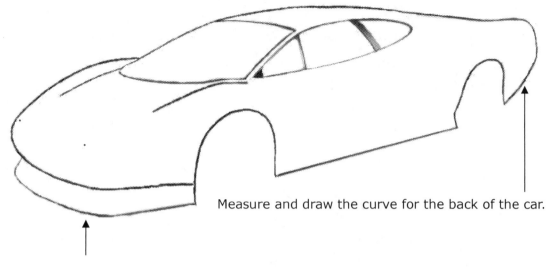

Measure and draw the curve for the back of the car.

Measure down from each of the two dots you made earlier to the
bottom line and draw a similar shape for the bottom front of the car.

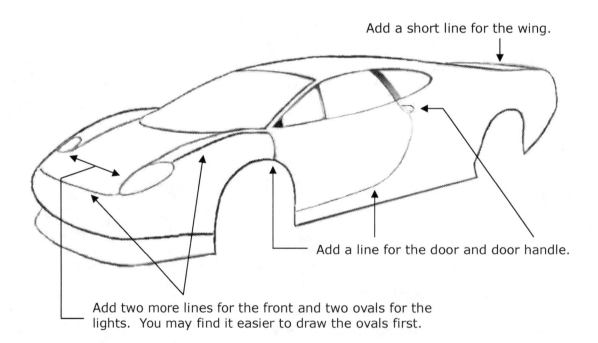

Add a short line for the wing.

Add a line for the door and door handle.

Add two more lines for the front and two ovals for the
lights. You may find it easier to draw the ovals first.

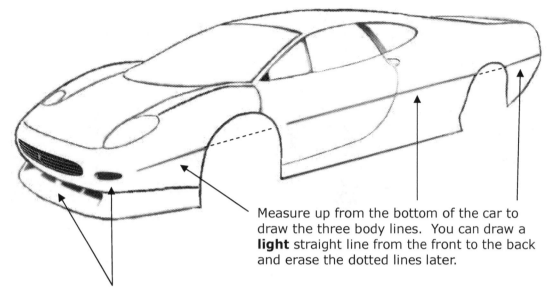

Measure up from the bottom of the car to draw the three body lines. You can draw a **light** straight line from the front to the back and erase the dotted lines later.

Shade in the details at the front of the car.

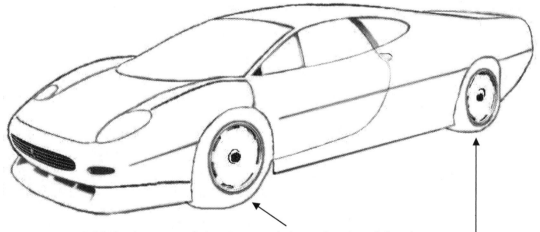

Add the bottom of the tires and draw the detail for the rims. For the rims draw a big circle inside the tire area with two smaller circles in the center of the big circle. Draw curved rectangular shapes just inside the big circle and then shade them in as shown above.

Draw the mirrors, windshield wiper and two
curved lines below the front windshield.

Draw an oval for the gas cap.

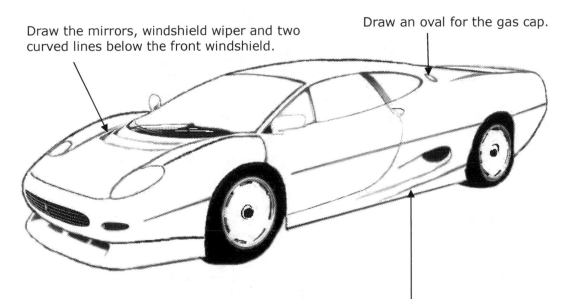

Add the side air intake and a small line in front of the back wheel as shown here.

Lamborghini Murciélago

General Information

Price:	$273,000 U.S.
Miles per Gallon:	13 mpg
Curb Weight:	3638 lbs
Layout:	Mid-Engine/AWD
Transmission:	6-Speed Manual

Engine

Type:	V12
Displacement:	6192 cc
Horsepower:	580 @ 7500 rpm
Torque:	480 lb-ft @ 5400 rpm

Performance

0-60 mph:	3.6 sec
0-100 mph:	8.7 sec
Quarter Mile:	12.0 sec @ 121 mph
Top Speed:	205 mph

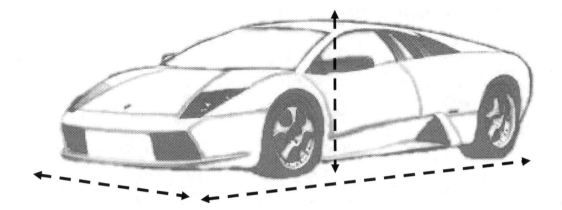

Measure the size of your area so you stay within your boundaries.

Start by measuring and drawing the top of the windshield.

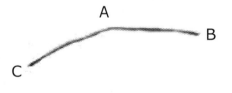

Measure and draw a line between pints "A" and "C"
for the left side of the windshield.

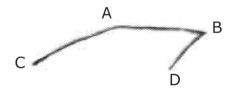

Measure between points "B" and "D" and draw the right side of the windshield.

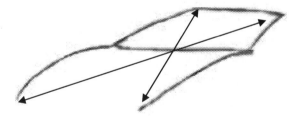

Now complete the bottom of the windshield but curve the line here. You can measure between the top left and right corners of the windshield to the curve to make sure you get the angle correct (see the arrows inside the windshield area).

Measure from the bottom of each corner of the windshield to the end of each of these lines and then draw the two front sides of the car.
Notice that the left line is curved and the right line is mostly straight with a curve close to the windshield. You can double check the angles by measuring between the arrows.

Draw a line to connect the front.

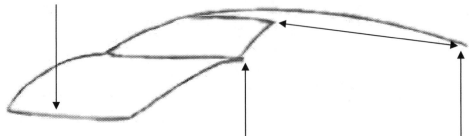

Measure straight back from the bottom right corner of the windshield to the back of the car (see arrows) and make a mark. Next draw the curved line for the roof from the top left corner of the windshield to the mark you made for the back of the car. Double check this by measuring from the top right of the windshield to the back of the car (see the double arrow).

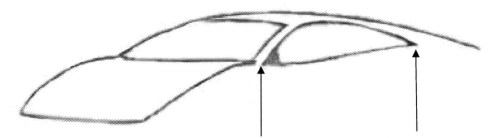

Measure between the arrows and draw the bottom of the side window. Now draw a curved line for the top of this window and add the shaded triangle at the front.

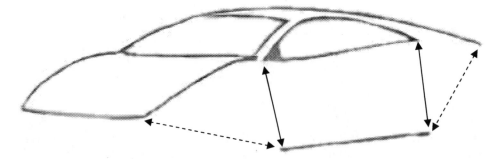

Measure from each end of the side window to the bottom of the car and then draw the line for the bottom of the car. You can double check this by measuring between the two dotted arrows.

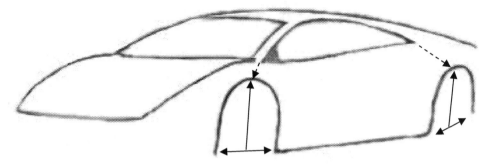

Measure between these points and make marks at the end of the arrows. Next draw half ovals for the wheel wells noticing that the back wheel well is angled upwards. You can double check the top of each wheel well by measuring from each end of the side window to the top of the wheel wells (see dotted arrows).

Draw the curved line to complete the back of the car.

Make two measurements between the double arrows to get the distance correct and then draw the curved lines to complete the bottom front of the car.

Measure and draw in the lines for the hood.

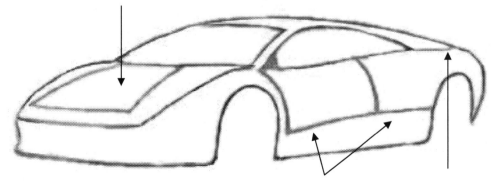

Draw the lines for the door and add the short line behind the side window.

Draw the bottom of the tires and circles for the main shape of the rims. Shade the inside detail of the rims (see the example below for the front rim). Notice that the back rim looks like it is right on the tire. This is because of the angle the car is facing.

Draw an oval for the outline of the rim.

Draw a half oval at the bottom inside of the last oval and then draw smaller circles and ovals for the general detail of the shaded areas.

Shade in the dark areas and add small dots just inside the bottom part of the rim.

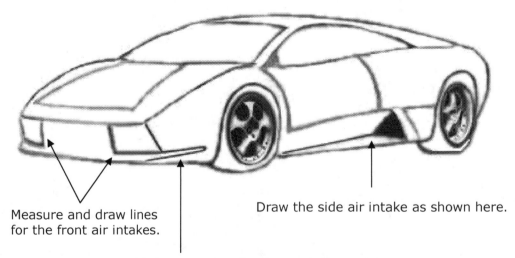

Measure and draw lines for the front air intakes.

Draw the side air intake as shown here.

Add the angle line for the air foil.

Add the final detail and shade where need. Now you can share your
drawing with all of your friends.

Ferrari Testarossa

General Information

Price:	$87,000 U.S.
Miles per Gallon:	15 mpg
Curb Weight:	3660 lbs
Layout:	Mid-Engine/RWD
Transmission:	5-Speed Manual

Engine

Type:	Flat 12
Displacement:	4942 cc
Horsepower:	390 @ 6300 rpm
Torque:	354 lb-ft @ 4500 rpm

Performance

0-60 mph:	5.3 sec
0-100 mph:	12.2 sec
Quarter Mile:	N/A
Top Speed:	180 mph

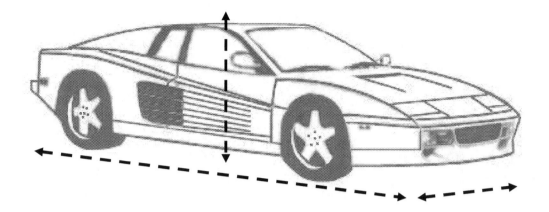

Measure the size of your area so you stay within your boundaries.

Measure and draw the top of the windshield. Make sure that the angles are correct otherwise your drawing will look bent.

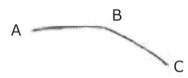

Measure between "B" and "C" and draw the right side of the windshield.

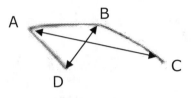

Measure between "A" and "D" and draw the line for the left side of the windshield. You can check the position of these lines by measuring from corner to corner (see arrows).

Connect the bottom of the windshield to complete it.

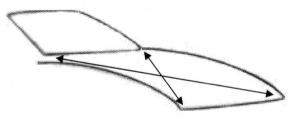

Draw the sides of the car and connect the front. The line for the front should be parallel to the top of the windshield. You can double check your angles by measuring between the arrows shown above.

Measure from the bottom left corner of the windshield to the back of the car and make a mark at the back of the car. Now draw a curved line from the mark at the back to the top right corner of the windshield.

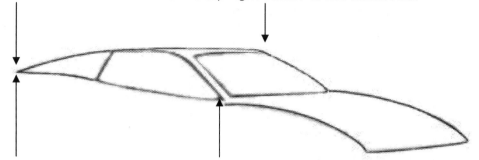

Draw a line form the front left side of the windshield to the back of the car (draw this line slightly curved). Add the small slanted vertical line to separate the window from the back.

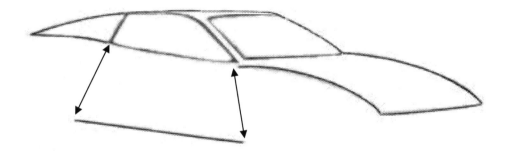

Measure between the double arrows and draw the bottom line.

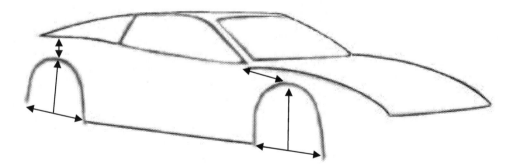

Measure between these points and draw a half oval for each wheel well. Check your measurements from the double arrows above the wheel wells.

Measure and extend the line for the back between the arrows.

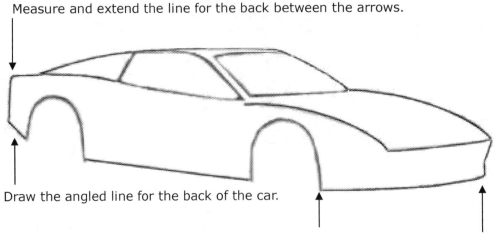

Draw the angled line for the back of the car.

Draw a curved line for the front between the front of the wheel well and the right side of the car (note the bend on the right side).

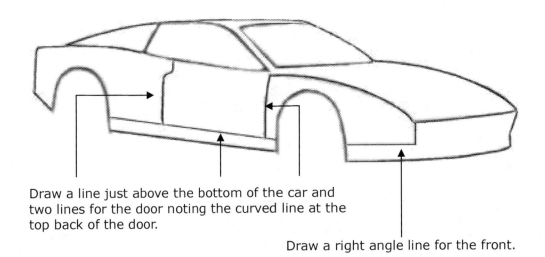

Draw a line just above the bottom of the car and two lines for the door noting the curved line at the top back of the door.

Draw a right angle line for the front.

Measure from the back of the front wheel well (see the dotted arrow) to the two points at the back of the car and then draw these two lines.

Draw another similar line above the line at the front.

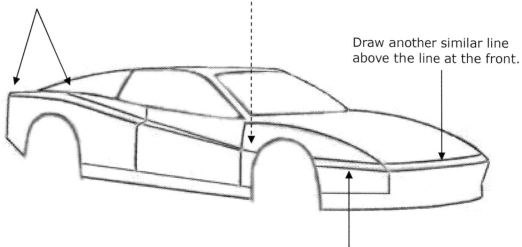

Continue the two lines from the front of the car along the side.

Add a small dot for the door lock.

Note the angle here.

Draw the lines for the bottom of the tires and fill them in by drawing the circles for the rims and triangles for the inside of the rims.

Draw lines for the front air intake and headlights.

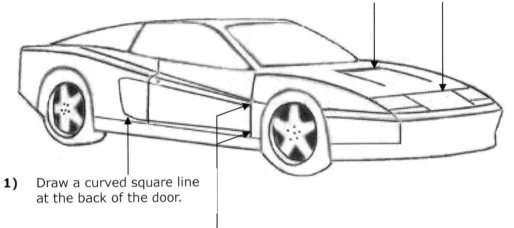

1) Draw a curved square line at the back of the door.

2) Draw two lines across the door at these points that join the curved square.

Add thick dark lines for the side window and draw two mirrors.

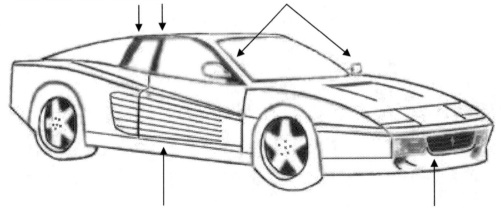

Add five lines for the side intake (if you can't fit five lines four will look just as good). To make it look good evenly space these lines apart and draw fine lines with a sharp pencil or mechanical pencil.

Shade in the details for the front.

Draw the back bumper.

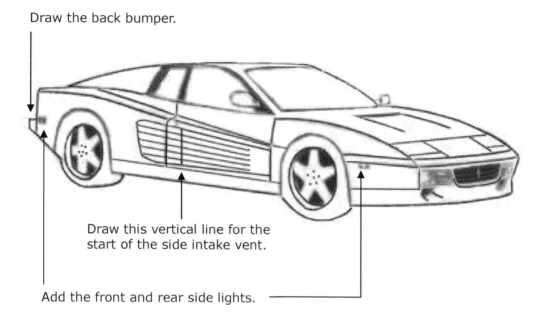

Draw this vertical line for the
start of the side intake vent.

Add the front and rear side lights.

Draw in the windshield wipers.

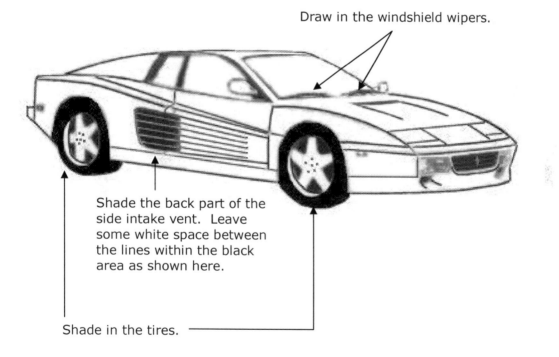

Shade the back part of the
side intake vent. Leave
some white space between
the lines within the black
area as shown here.

Shade in the tires.

Lotus Esprit

General Information

Price:	$85,000 + U.S.
Miles per Gallon:	20 mpg
Curb Weight:	2968 lbs
Layout:	Mid-Engine/RWD
Transmission:	5-Speed Manual

Engine

Type:	Twin-Turbo V8
Displacement:	3500 cc
Horsepower:	350 @ 6500 rpm
Torque:	295 lb-ft @ 4250 rpm

Performance

0-60 mph:	4.4 sec
0-100 mph:	11.0 sec
Quarter Mile:	13.0 sec @ 112 mph
Top Speed:	175 mph

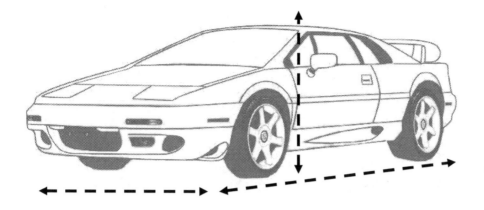

Measure the size of your area so you stay within your boundaries.

A ————————— B

Start by drawing the top of the windshield.

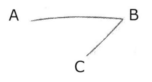

A ————————— B

C

Draw the right side of the windshield by measuring between "B" and "C". Double check this angle by measuring between "A" and "C".

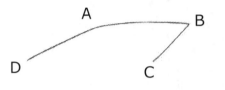

Draw the left side of the windshield by measuring between "A" and "D". Double check this angle by measuring between "B" and "D".

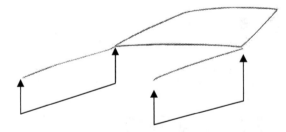

Connect the bottom of the windshield. Double check your angles by measuring between the arrows.

Measure the lines from each bottom corner of the windshield to the end of the lights and draw these two lines.

3)   Draw a curved line starting just to the right of the top right corner of the windshield to the mark you just made in step 2. Now draw another line connecting the top front of the side window to the bottom as shown. Note that the bottom of the side window is curved.

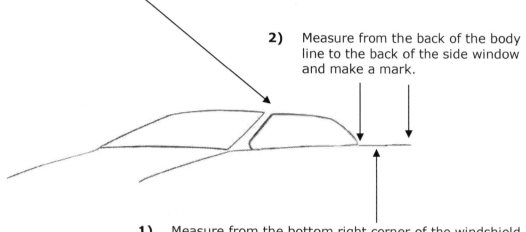

2)   Measure from the back of the body line to the back of the side window and make a mark.

1)   Measure from the bottom right corner of the windshield to the back of the car and draw the top body line.

Draw the roof line **above** the top left of the windshield to the arrow here.

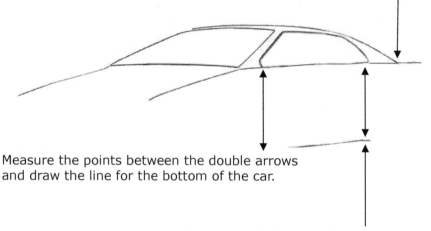

Measure the points between the double arrows and draw the line for the bottom of the car.

Note the bend at the back of the bottom line.

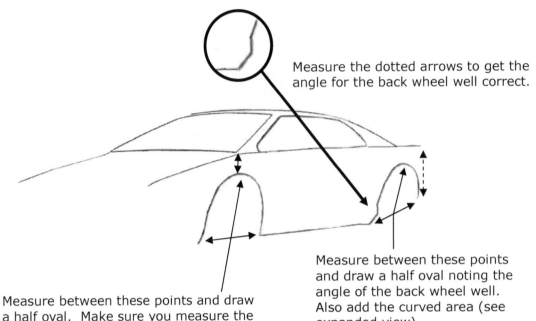

Measure the dotted arrows to get the angle for the back wheel well correct.

Measure between these points and draw a half oval noting the angle of the back wheel well. Also add the curved area (see expanded view).

Measure between these points and draw a half oval. Make sure you measure the double arrow from the windshield to the top of the wheel well.

Draw a line between the arrows from the top left of the windshield to the front of the car close to the existing lines but not touching.

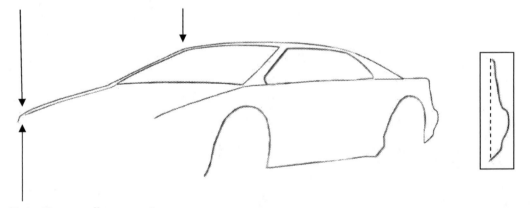

Note the small curve at the end of this line.

Draw the curved line for the back of the car. You might find it easier to draw a **light** line straight down and then add the bent part later (see the expanded view at the right). You can erase the **light** line and darken the curved line later.

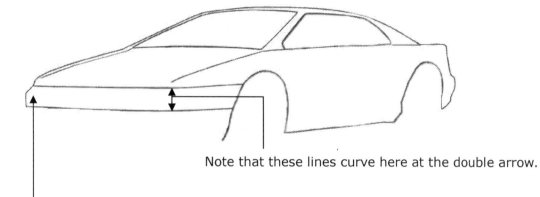

Note that these lines curve here at the double arrow.

Draw the two curved lines for the front of the car. Draw
the top line first noting the small angle at the left.

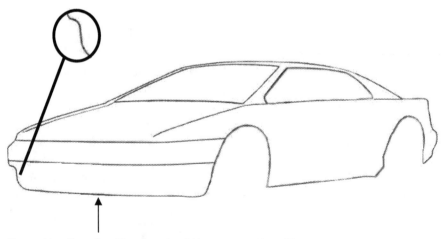

Draw the line for the front of the car noting the
curved line at the left (see the expanded view).

Draw in the lines for the hood.

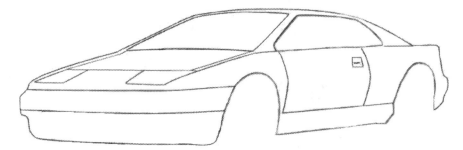

Draw in the lines for the door and door handle.

Add the short line at the back.

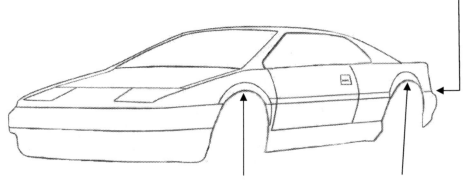

Add the lines above the wheel wells and through the center of the body.

Measure and draw the wing as shown.

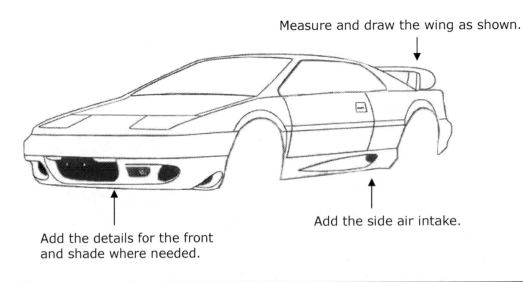

Add the side air intake.

Add the details for the front
and shade where needed.

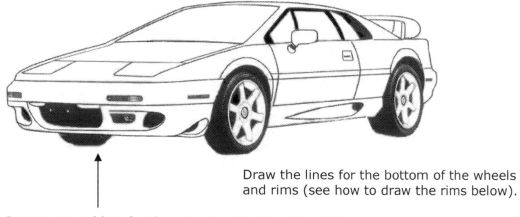

Draw the lines for the bottom of the wheels and rims (see how to draw the rims below).

Draw a curved line for the wheel on the far side of the car.

The front and back rims are similar.

Draw three circles inside each other.

Draw a half circle inside the bigger circle.

Draw triangles for the dark areas.

Shade in the black areas. Add the mirror, black lines for the side window and the other lights.

Ferrari F50

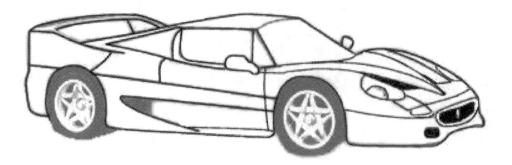

General Information

Price:	$1,430,000 U.S.
Miles per Gallon:	N/A
Curb Weight:	2005 lbs
Layout:	Mid-Engine/RWD
Transmission:	6-Speed Sequential

Engine

Type:	V12
Displacement:	4700 cc
Horsepower:	680 @ 10,500 rpm
Torque:	383 lb-ft @ 8000 rpm

Performance

0-60 mph:	3.8 sec
0-100 mph:	6.7 sec
Quarter Mile:	11.2 sec @ 129 mph
Top Speed:	202 mph

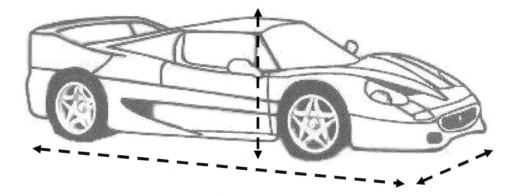

Measure the area for your boundaries to start your drawing.

Draw the top of the windshield. Measure straight across and make marks for the ends of the line and then draw a curved line between these points.

Measure and draw the right side of the windshield. You can check your angle by measuring from the top left of the windshield to the bottom right side of windshield.

Measure and draw the left side of the windshield. Again you can check the angle by measuring from the top right side of the windshield to the bottom left of the windshield.

Finish the bottom of the windshield with a curved line. Draw this line lightly as you may need to erase and correct it later.

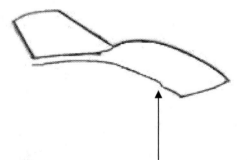

Draw two curved lines for the fenders and then joint the front together. Note the small curve in the left fender line. Draw this line **lightly** and correct it later if needed.

1) Complete the top of the side window and add the two vertical lines. Next add the angled line from the back of the side window to the back of the car.

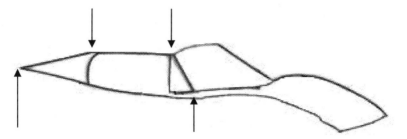

2) Continue the curved body line between these points.

Draw the curved roof line between these points.

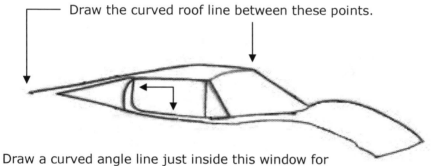

Draw a curved angle line just inside this window for the glass (see the arrows inside the window).

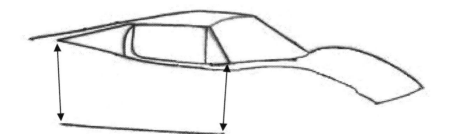

Measure between these points and draw the line for the bottom of the car.

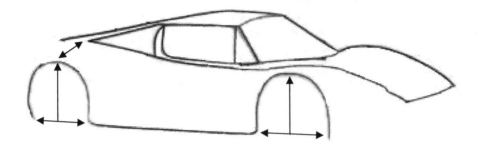

Measure between these points and draw the wheel wells.

Measure these points for a correct measurement
for the side of the back wing and extend the
front of this line just under the side window.

Measure between the arrows to make
sure the distance for the front is correct.

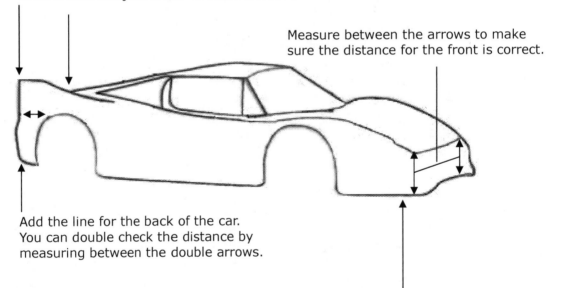

Add the line for the back of the car.
You can double check the distance by
measuring between the double arrows.

Add the front and side lines.
Measure carefully for the front curved line
noting the shape of the front of the car.

Complete the back wing.

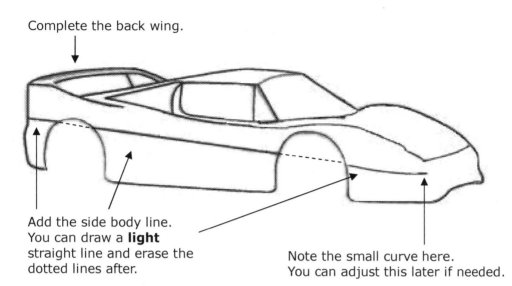

Add the side body line.
You can draw a **light**
straight line and erase the
dotted lines after.

Note the small curve here.
You can adjust this later if needed.

Add this small curved line for the engine compartment.

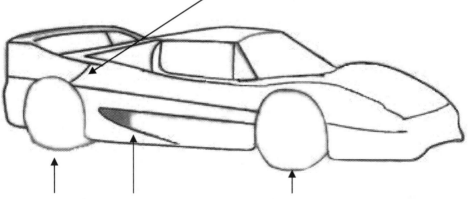

Draw the bottom of the wheels and the side intake vent.

Add the lines for the lights and other small lines for the front.

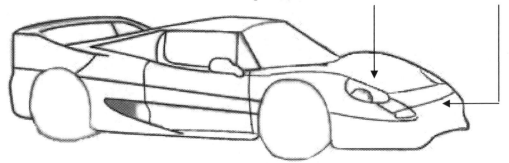

Add the lines for the door and mirror.

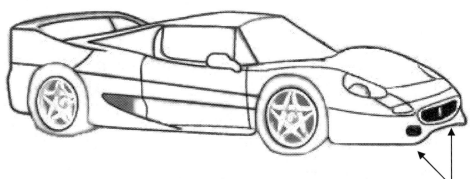

Add a circle for each rim and triangles
shapes for the inside of the rims then
shade in the triangles as shown.

Shade in the details for the front.

Add the other mirror and lines for the hood noting the angles of the hood lines.

Shade the tires and other needed areas and enjoy your masterpiece.

Porsche 959

General Information

Price: $247,000 U.S.
Miles per Gallon: 13 mpg
Curb Weight: 3199 lbs
Layout: Rear-Engine/AWD
Transmission: 6-Speed Manual

Engine

Type: Twin-Turbo Flat-6
Displacement: 2851 cc
Horsepower: 450 bhp @ 6500 rpm
Torque: 370 lb-ft @ 5500 rpm

Performance

0-60 mph: 3.7 sec
0-100 mph: 8.3 sec
Quarter Mile: 11.8 sec @ 123 mph
Top Speed: 190 mph

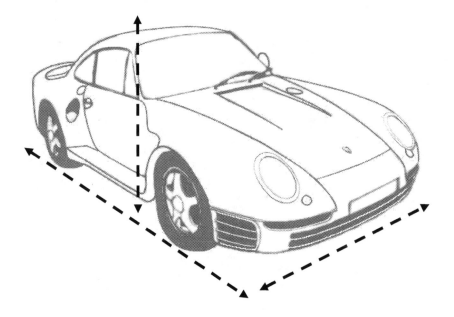

Start with measuring for the area of the car.

Measure and draw the line for the top of the windshield.

Measure and draw the right side of the windshield.

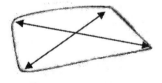

Measure and draw the left side of the windshield.

The completed windshield should look similar to this. Double check your measurements by measuring between the arrows.

Measure from each bottom corner of the windshield to the end of these lines and make a mark for each line at the end. Next draw the lines for the hood from the bottom of the windshield to your marks being careful the curve is correct.

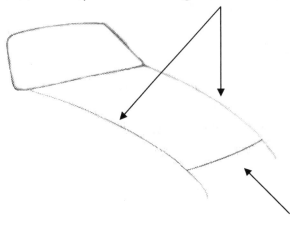

Measure up from each end of these lines and draw a line across the front as shown.

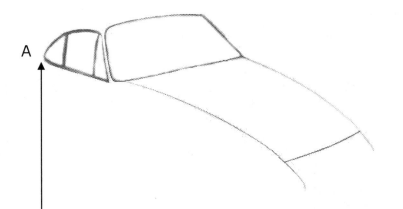

A

Measure from the bottom left corner of the windshield to point "A" and draw the bottom of the side window. Next draw the curved line for the top of the side window and the vertical lines inside it. Measure the height of the side window from the bottom line at different points to get the height and curve correct.

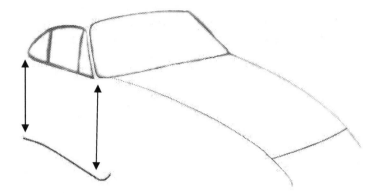

Measure between the arrows and then draw the line for the bottom of the car. Note the small curl at the front of this line and a small bend at the back.

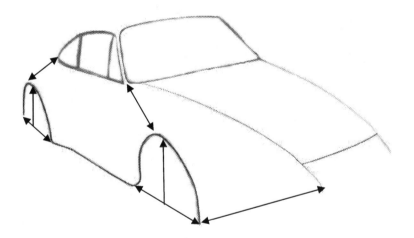

Measure between these points and draw the ovals for the wheel wells.

Add the curved line for the roof between these points. Measure from the top left corner of the windshield straight up to the roof line and make a mark to get the curve correct.

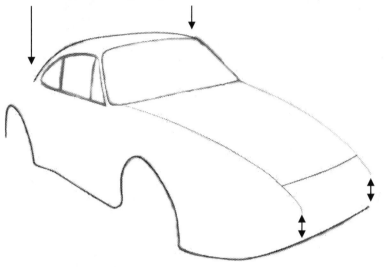

Add the curved line for the front of the car. Measure between the double arrows to make sure the distance is correct.

Draw a curved line for the back of the car and the start of the wing.

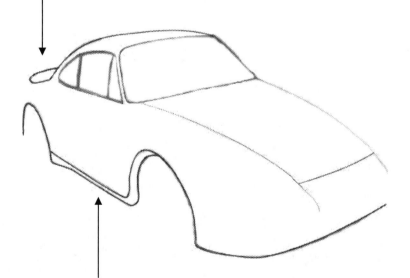

Add a second line just above the bottom of the car and curve it up to the front wheel well.

Draw a curved line up from the back wheel
well to the roof to create the back wing.

Draw a curved line from the corner of
the windshield to the bottom front of
the car. Measure between the double
arrows to assure your curve is correct.

Add another curved line for the front fender.

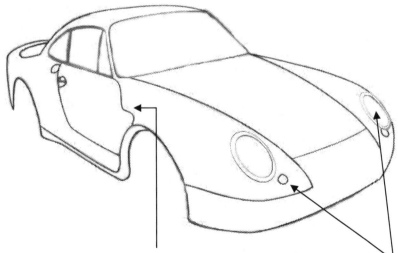

Draw the lines for the door and the door handle.
Note the squiggle line for the front of the door.

Add six ovals for the front lights.

Add a small oval and then shade
part of it in for the side intake.

Draw a small half oval for the mirror.

Draw the lines for the hood intake
and a circle for the gas door.

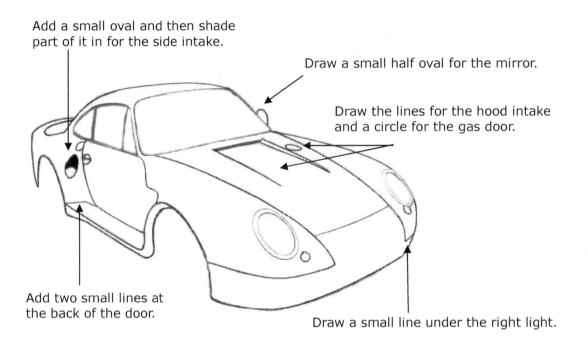

Add two small lines at
the back of the door.

Draw a small line under the right light.

Add an extra line below the
wing for the back of the car.

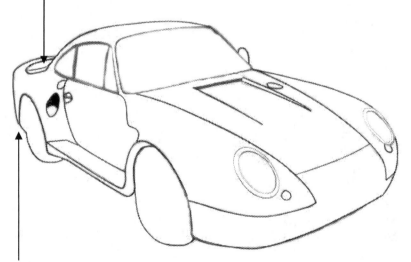

Add the lines for the bottom of the tires.
Note the bent part at the back tire (see arrow).

Add two curved lines for the windshield wipers.

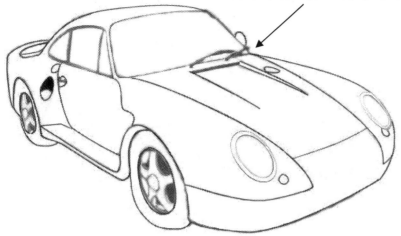

Fill in the details for the rims using circles and ovals with black curved triangles. The angle of this picture only shows ¾ of the back rim.

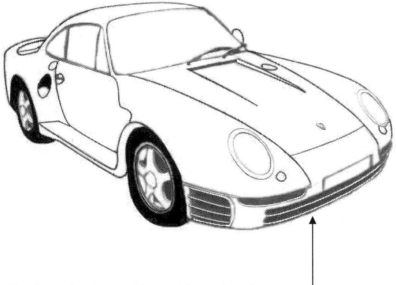

Shade in the tires, side and front details.

TIP: For the side and front details draw fine lines for the white lines and then shade around them as shown. This is similar to the Ferrari Testarossa side door vents.

Vector M12

General Information

Price:	$284,000 U.S.
Miles per Gallon:	N/A
Curb Weight:	3320 lbs
Layout:	Mid-Engine/RWD
Transmission:	3-Speed Automatic

Engine

Type:	Twin-Turbo V8
Displacement:	6000 cc
Horsepower:	525 bhp @ 5700 rpm
Torque:	360 lb-ft @ 4800 rpm

Performance

0-60 mph:	4.5 sec
0-100 mph:	8.3 sec
Quarter Mile:	12.0 sec @ 124 mph
Top Speed:	218 mph

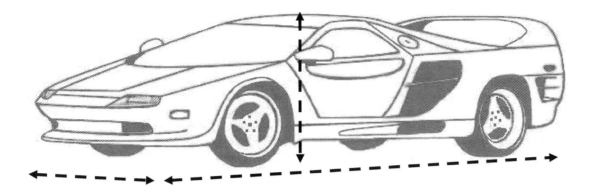

Make your area measurements and then start one of
the world's most awesome super cars.

Start with the top of the windshield.

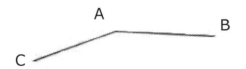

Draw the line for the left side of the windshield by measuring between "A" and
"C". Double check your angle by measuring between "B" and "C".

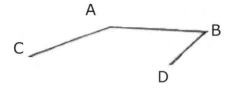

Draw the right side of the windshield by measuring between "B" and "D".
Double check the angle by measuring between "A" and "D".

Add the curved line for the bottom of the windshield and shade the left corner.

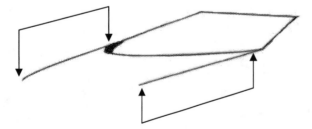

Measure between these points and draw the two side lines for the hood.

Measure from the top left corner of the windshield to the back of the car and draw this curved line. Double check the angle by measuring the dotted arrows.

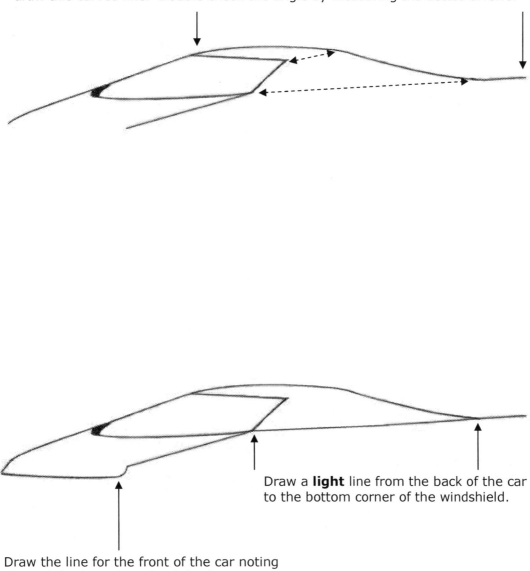

Draw a **light** line from the back of the car to the bottom corner of the windshield.

Draw the line for the front of the car noting the curl on the right side of this line.

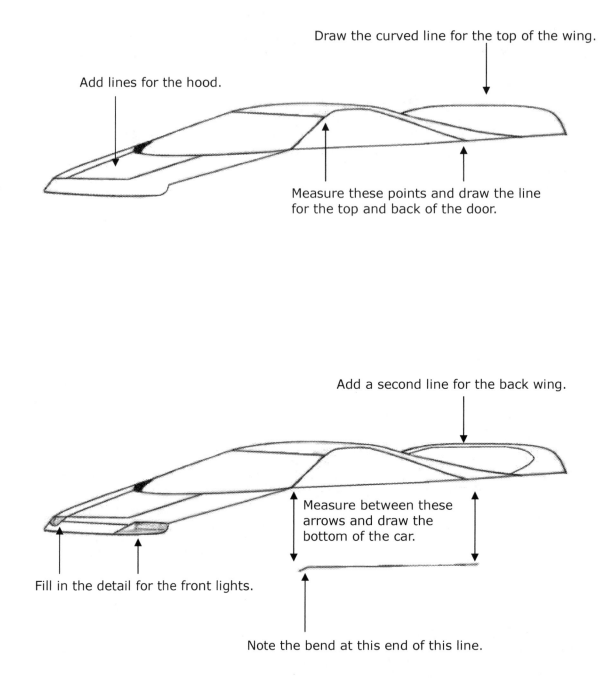

Draw the curved line for the top of the wing.

Add lines for the hood.

Measure these points and draw the line for the top and back of the door.

Add a second line for the back wing.

Measure between these arrows and draw the bottom of the car.

Fill in the detail for the front lights.

Note the bend at this end of this line.

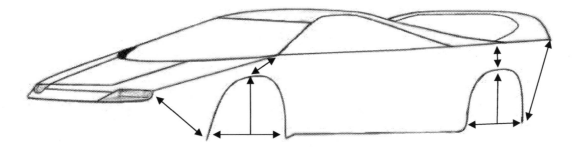

Measure these points and draw the lines for the wheel wells.

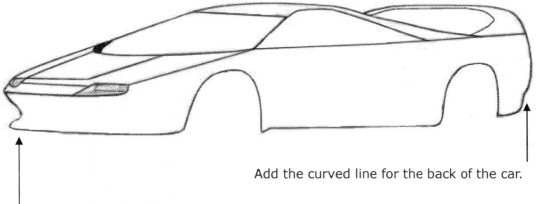

Add the curved line for the back of the car.

Add the front of the car noting the
curved shape on the left side of this line.

Erase the line between the dotted arrows.

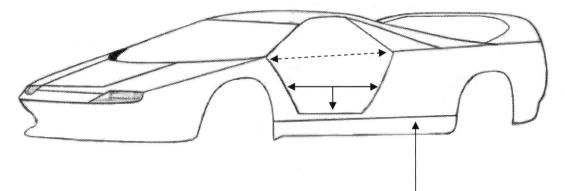

Draw the lines for the door (three way arrow) and another line just below the door.

Add the door mirrors and two door windows.

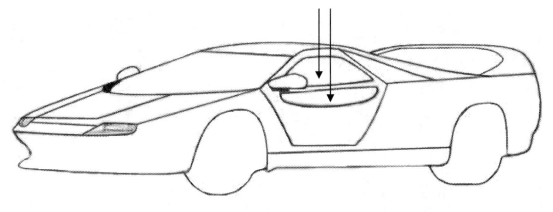

Draw the lines for the tires noting where they attach to the car.

Shade this inner part of the wing.

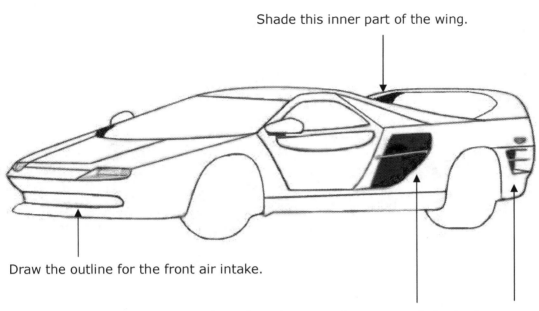

Draw the outline for the front air intake.

Draw the side and rear intake vents and shade them in.
Add the back light and the line above the rear intake vent.

Add a circle inside each rim and rounded triangles for the inside detail.

Draw an oval for the gas door.

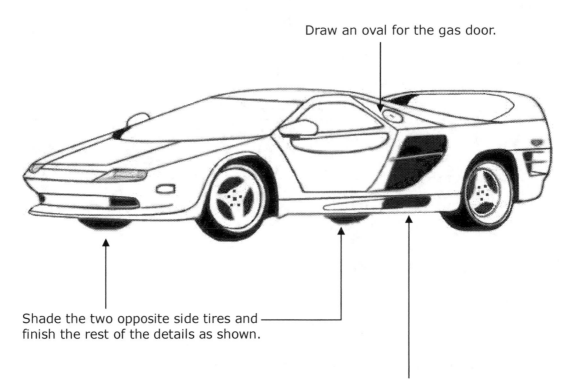

Shade the two opposite side tires and
finish the rest of the details as shown.

Add the small intake vent at the bottom of the car.

You are now on your way to use these skills for drawing other cars and more. Using the method you learned in this book find other pictures to draw breaking them down into parts or steps as described in this book. Remember to first measure the whole area your picture will use. Always start with light lines and check your angles as you go.

I sincerely hope you had fun learning this drawing technique. By practicing these skills there is no telling what you can draw.

Printed in the United States
by Baker & Taylor Publisher Services